Brace Yourself for ...ther Day

Ginnell McDonald

Brace Yourself for Another Day
Copyright © 2019 Ginnell McDonald

Story and illustrations by Ginnell McDonald

A special thank you to Tina Hallis for her help with this book.

ISBN 9781704112008
Library of Congress Control Number 2019918957

To Dennis, Nicholas, and
Kevin, who help me get through
my everyday challenges.
Forever love to you.

Muscular Dystrophy is a
genetic disorder that weakens
the muscles that help the
body move.

Courtesy of Kids Health, 2013

All proceeds from this book will be
donated to the Muscular Dystrophy
Association

Oh no! It's 7:15 and I am late! The old yellow school bus waits under my favorite maple tree. The door cranks open and there sits Bert, the bus driver.

He is a kind man. He has a balding head and small round glasses. Every morning he greets me. He says, "Good morning Peaches. It's going to be a great day!"

I used to be able to jump on the bus and skip down the aisle to my seat. When we'd get to school, I'd bounce down the steps and jump onto a patch of soft green grass. Then I would run to be first in line.

But not anymore. I had to get leg braces. What are they?
Why did I have to have them? I was told that I have
muscular dystrophy, and that the muscles in my legs need
help to walk. I wondered how the braces were ever going to
help me. They were hard, heavy, and stiff. They cramped
my feet! And worst of all, I had to wear special shoes!

When I got those special shoes, I would lace them up and head for the garage. I would look for Big Blue. Big Blue was an old blue bike my dad picked up at a rummage sale. It was a one-speed with fat tires and a large balloon-like seat.

I would get on Big Blue and pedal down the street as fast as I could go. Then I would drag my toes on the sidewalk and try to destroy those shoes! I wanted so much to have pretty shoes.

Every stop Bert made, beautiful shoes would climb aboard.

There were shoes with glitter, sparkles, buckles, and even rainbow-colored shoe laces! I wanted to wear beautiful shoes.

The bus is approaching the schoolyard. I let all the other kids get off the bus first.

Clump! Clump! Clump! One step at a time, I step off the bus, looking for the curb. I take a deep breath and get ready for the challenges of the day.

First, there is the school building. My school has lots of steps but no elevator.

I think it would be

And a fast, curvy slide that zoomed

down to the lunchroom.

In the winter, there is no place to put on and take off your boots.

I wish each locker could be transformed into a throne.

It would be a place to sit, change your shoes, and start your day feeling like a king or queen.

When my class sits on the carpet to listen to a story, I worry about not being able to get up.

I wish I had an inflatable chair that would help me stand. It would shoot me into the air like a rocket! How fun would that be?

Recess is another challenge. You know all the "ing" words like skipping, running, jumping, and chasing? Well, they're not so fun for me! Wouldn't it be wonderful to have a playground where paintbrushes grew in the grass and paint dripped from the trees?

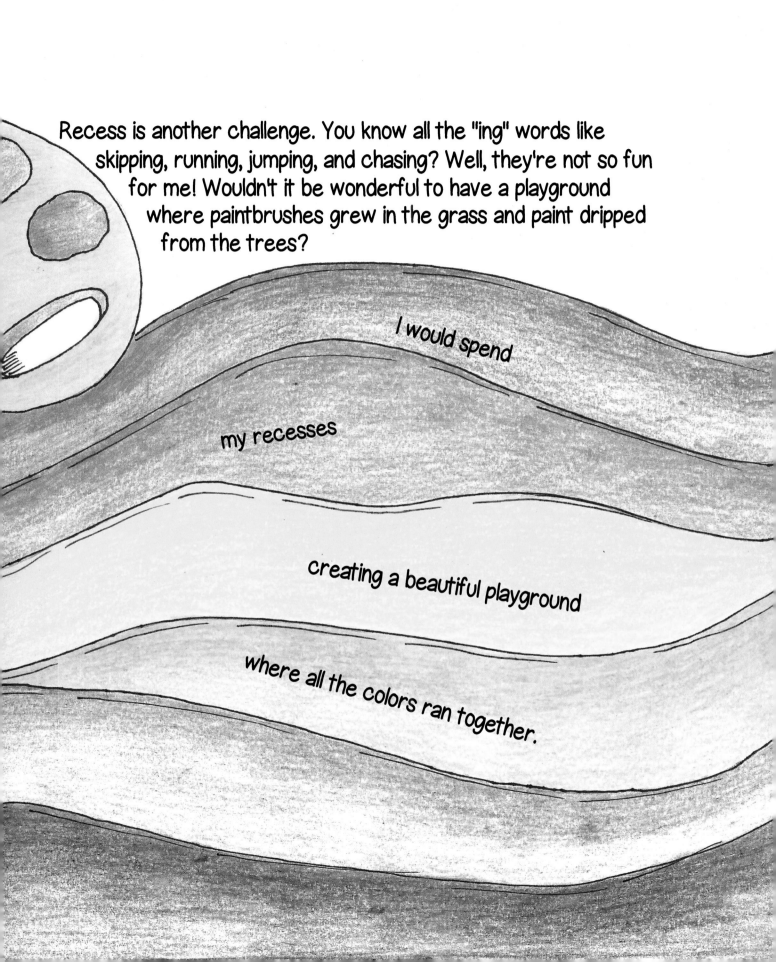

I would spend

my recesses

creating a beautiful playground

where all the colors ran together.

Finally, there is the dreaded gym class. I wish I could write to the P.E. angels and have them sprinkle magical dust on my legs to help me do all those "ing" things.

My dreams and wishes make me smile. But I know my braces are the real things that help me through the challenges I face every day.

When I wake up in the morning, I try to be the best I can be and celebrate the things that I can do. The truth is I really depend on those braces to get me through each day. Maybe they're not so bad after all.

In fact, they are kind of like a BFF (best friend forever). They have many BFF traits.

They are trustworthy, loyal, and dependable. They won't let me fall, they stick with me no matter what, and they are forgiving even though I don't always treat them nicely.

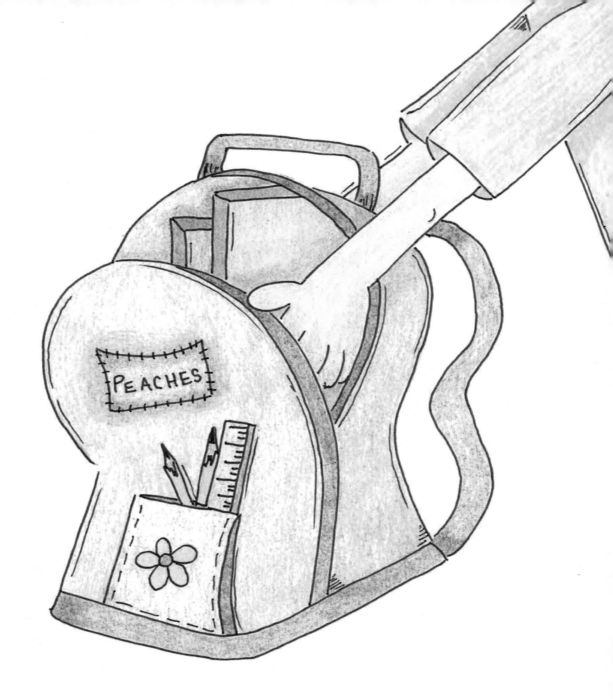

As I get ready to go home, I see Bert pull up in front of the school. Well, I did make it through another day.

Bert was right, it was a great day. But I couldn't have done it without my BFF braces!

The End

Made in the USA
Monee, IL
25 June 2022

98622842R00019